William A Spicer

The High School Boys of the Tenth R.I. Regiment

With a Roll of Teachers and Students of the Providence High School....

William A Spicer

The High School Boys of the Tenth R.I. Regiment
With a Roll of Teachers and Students of the Providence High School....

ISBN/EAN: 9783337211752

Printed in Europe, USA, Canada, Australia, Japan

Cover: Foto ©ninafisch / pixelio.de

More available books at **www.hansebooks.com**

THE HIGH SCHOOL BOYS

OF THE

TENTH R. I. REGIMENT,

WITH A

ROLL OF TEACHERS AND STUDENTS

OF THE PROVIDENCE HIGH SCHOOL,

WHO SERVED IN THE ARMY OR NAVY OF THE UNITED STATES
DURING THE REBELLION.

BY

WILLIAM A. SPICER,

COMPANY B, TENTH RHODE ISLAND VOLUNTEERS.

———◆———

PROVIDENCE:
N. BANGS WILLIAMS & COMPANY
1882.

THE HIGH SCHOOL BOYS

OF THE

TENTH R I REGIMENT

———◆———

OUR school days were cast in eventful times.
Some of the Providence boys who met twenty years
ago, in the old High School on Benefit street, can
hardly have forgotten the stirring events which pre-
ceded the war, and the memorable presidential cam-
paign of 1860, when they joined the Lincoln wide-
awake army, proudly shouldered their torches and
marched on to victory, little heeding the threatening
clouds of secession gathering in the Southern hori-
zon. How few then, at the North, young or old,
realized the nearness of the storm which was soon to
burst forth and rage for four long years, carrying
blight and desolation into almost every family in the
land. A struggle which cost the lives of more than

half a million brave men, and cost the nation also,
during the last year, more than three million dollars
a day! and left it, at last, with a debt of more than
two billion seven hundred millions!

The excitement which followed the attack on Fort
Sumpter, in April, 1861, was fully shared by the
High School boys. Every one was expected to show
his colors, and it was voted to purchase and raise the
national flag over the High School building. Hearing that the college boys were about to unfurl the stars
and stripes over University Hall, (where, eighty-
eight years before, the old Revolutionary flag had
floated,) it was determined to get the start of them,
if possible. Wednesday afternoon, April 17th, at
five o'clock, being the time appointed for the exercises at the college, the following High School announcement appeared in the *Journal* of that day:
" The 'stars and stripes' will be raised this afternoon
from the High School, at *half past four!*" But the
boys were finally induced to defer their public demon-
stration till the following morning, though they
couldn't refrain from indulging in a little informal
raising, at the hour first announced, thus securing

the desired priority, and the following notice from the *Evening Press:* "High School Patriotism.—A splendid national flag, purchased by the subscription of over one hundred High School boys, was displayed from the High School building, this afternoon!" The formal exercises next morning were of a most interesting character. At eleven o'clock, in the presence of teachers, scholars, citizens, and soldiers about leaving for the war, the boys raised the flag, followed by the singing of the "Star Spangled Banner." The young ladies of the school carried small national flags. Mayor Knight delivered a brief opening address, and introduced Professor Chace, of Brown University, who responded with scholarly and patriotic sentiments. Bishop Clark related an anecdote of his great grandfather, who, after the battle of Bunker Hill, was obliged to sleep in a baker's oven, and added, "I am glad that he did not get *baked*, else I should not have been here to-day to address you!" and turning to the "Marines," who were to leave that afternoon for Washington, with the 1st Rhode Island regiment, he said, "some of *you* may have to sleep in a baker's oven before you get back, but I hope you will not get baked, but live to come home well bre(a)d men, as you now are." They were indeed soon tried in the fiery furnace of Bull Run, and some never returned. Ex-Mayor Rodman, in his pleasant manner, referred to a conversation between General Nathanael Greene and his mother, during the Revolution, in which she cautioned him "not to get shot in the back!" Dr. Caldwell made an impressive closing address, when "America" was heartily sung, followed by cheers for "the Union," "the young ladies of the High School," "Governor Sprague," the "First Regiment," and the "Marines." "Fifteen cheers and a Narragansett" were also served up by the boys for a dispatch read by Bishop Clark, "that Virginia had decided not to secede." But they found out, a few days later, that they had wasted their ammunition.

It was now apparent that there was sufficient military spirit to warrant the formation of a High School company A meeting was held in the hall, at which a committee of arrangements was appointed, and in a few weeks the boys fell into line under the name of the "Ellsworth Phalanx," in honor of the youthful and gallant commander of the New York

Zouaves, who had been shot at Alexandria, Va., May 24th, while engaged in lowering a rebel flag from a hotel in that city How it would have startled the members of the Ellsworth Phalanx, had they been told that in the next year some of their number would be marching through that same rebellious city, and by the very hotel where Ellsworth fell! but so it proved, the boys singing " Ellsworth Avengers" with a will, and "John Brown's Body," as they went "marching on."

The beautiful standard of colors presented to the Phalanx, was the gift of the young ladies of the High School. Daniel W. Lyman, late our accomplished senator in the assembly from North Providence, was chosen captain. An arrangement was made with the United Train of Artillery by which their armory on Canal street became the headquarters of the corps, which, under the direction of the veteran Colonel Wescott Handy, of the Old Guard Continentals, soon attained a creditable degree of proficiency Those were refreshing seasons; who can forget them? when, after the long and toilsome drill, or street parade, good Col. Handy marched us through his root and herb beer establishment, near the Great Bridge, and treated one and all to a large glass of his celebrated beer, "compounded strictly from medicinal roots and herbs." May his memory *ever* remain as fragrant as his *beer!* What wonder that the corps rapidly advanced in discipline and spirits, and soon attracted not a little public attention for its *steady* and soldierly bearing on parade. Its brilliant evening receptions, also, and exhibition drills, will be pleasantly recalled. How they enlivened the long winter evenings of '61!

But the Rebellion was not yet subdued. Brighter days were looked for with the opening of '62, but May came, and with it fresh news of disaster to the Union cause. Stonewall Jackson had sent Banks whirling down the Shenandoah Valley, to the Potomac, and at midnight, on the 25th, a dispatch came to Providence announcing the disaster with an urgent appeal for troops for the protection of the capitol. Just an hour later the Governor issued an order to immediately organize a new regiment, the Tenth Rhode Island volunteers, for three months' service. The response was prompt, and among other military organizations, the Ellsworth Phalanx contributed a liberal quota. The regiment was principally drawn from a volunteer organization of the citizens of Providence, known as the "National Guards," Colonel James Shaw, Jr., commanding, who was instructed by the regiment to offer its services "as then officered and organized." But Colonel Shaw, though an able and accomplished officer, felt that the chief command should be given to one who had received a military education; whereupon the Governor appointed Captain Z. R. Bliss, of the regular service, colonel of the Tenth, and James Shaw, Jr., lieutenant-colonel. By seven o'clock P. M., of the day of the call, 613 men were reported ready for duty; and the day following, the 27th, the Tenth regiment, under the command of Lieutenant-Colonel Shaw, left for Washington, Colonel Bliss being detained at home on account of his father's death. At the head of Company B, recruited almost entirely from the ranks of the High School and University companies, marched Captain Elisha Dyer, formerly Governor of the state. The men are few, who, at his age, (over fifty,) would have abandoned the comforts of home for the arduous position of captain in a volunteer regiment. *Most* of the permanent officers were gentlemen well known to the men, including Lieutenant-Colonel James Shaw, Jr., afterwards Colonel ; Major Jacob Babbitt of Bristol, killed at Fredericksburg the following December ; Adjutant John F. Tobey ; Dr. George W Wilcox, surgeon, and Rev. A. H. Clapp, the honored pastor of the Beneficent Church, chaplain. Hon. Nelson W Aldrich, our able senator in congress, was then, at the age of twenty-two, a member of Company D, and Hon. Joshua M. Addeman, secretary of state, a private in our student Company, B. And we would not forget, also, to honor the name of our youthful and lamented comrade, Frederick Metcalf, son of the worthy President of this Society. Although but fifteen years of age, he enlisted with his older classmates in Company B ; but Captain Dyer was unwilling to assume the responsibility of accepting so young a volunteer in the absence of his father, (then in active service with his regiment at Hilton Head, S. C.) But this did not dampen the ardor of young Metcalf, and we find him in October of the following year, a second lieutenant in his father's regiment. He also creditably served as Post Adjutant at Fort Pulaski, Georgia, till May 27, 1864, when he was promoted to a first lieutenancy. But in the following August he was attacked by a malarial fever. On the 19th of the month, seeming considerably better, he was removed for better care, to Beaufort, S. C. But there he gradually grew worse, and died on the 28th of August, in the seventeenth year of his age. His funeral was attended with full military honors. Though hardly a year in the army, he had won the respect of all his associates, and had earned one promotion in the field. Cut off in the dew of youth, he has left a memory forevermore associated with the most unselfish patriotism and pure devotion to duty

Those High School boys whose fortunate lot it was to be members of Captain Dyer's company, will hardly again find in life a day of such strange excitement as that in which they first put on uniform and started for camp.

Of the departure of the regiment, and the journey to Washington, others have told. The same enthusiasm greeted the Tenth as all the Rhode Island regiments. Who can forget the hearty reception in Philadelphia, at the rooms of the Volunteer Relief Association, or we of the Second Detachment, the midnight march through Baltimore, the rebellious city? Every man provided with several rounds of ball-cartridges, in case of trouble! Arriving at length at the capitol, the regiment had an immediate taste of army life, in the repulsive fare and quarters of the Soldiers' Retreat; but orders soon came to move, and on the 30th, an intensely hot day, marched to Tenallytown Village, six miles away, and went into camp.

From this point of the narrative, in an attempt to revive the memories of our three months' adventures, from their Rip Van Winkle slumber of twenty years, the writer has relied chiefly upon his old package of letters, preserved by his mother, extracts from which are now given, substantially as written.

Camp Frieze, near Tenallytown, D. C., June 3d and 4th, 1862. "To-day is a rainy one in camp, and the boys are either asleep, writing home, or lie stretched out on the straw, so I thought I'd give an account of our whereabouts. Camp Frieze, named in honor of the quartermaster-general of Rhode Island, is beautifully laid out in a grove of oak trees, with tents in parallel rows, and streets or avenues between. Ours is, of course, Dyer avenue. The Second ward company, D, have Benefit street. The Seventh ward company, Broadway, and the Sixth ward company, Atwood avenue, in honor of Mrs. Alice Atwood, of that ward, who made and presented the men with one hundred pin-cushions, filled with pins. William Grant and Ira Wilbur are in that company. The college boys of Co. B have named their quarters 'Hope College.' In our High School tent there are seventeen of us, as follows: 4th Sergeant Charles L. Stafford, Corporal William P Vaughan, and high privates Edwin B. Fiske, John A. Reynolds, Frank Frost, James F. Field, George T.* and Nathan H. Baker,* John B. Kelly,* Frank F Tingley, Charles B. and Charles T. Greene, George H. Sparhawk, H. K. Blanchard, David Hunt, Jesse M. Bush and myself—all in one Sibley tent! Ned. Glezen, Daniel Bush, Howard Sturges and Brock. Mathewson are in Co. D, and Zeph. Brown and Jesse Eddy in Co. K. We arrange ourselves round, at

* Promoted to be corporals.

night, like the spokes of a wheel, with our feet, or, as the army shoes are termed, 'whangs,' to the centre pole, around which our guns are stacked. We sleep on straw beds on the ground, spread our rubber blankets to keep off the dampness, and make our knapsacks serve as pillows. The rations thus far have been horrid; especially the meat, or 'salt horse'; so that Frank Tingley and I have been out two or three times to get a good square meal, for *only* twenty-five cents, at a neighboring farm house. The surrounding hill tops are covered with forts and batteries. Near us are Forts Pennsylvania, Slocum and Franklin, which command the roads leading to Harper's Ferry and Frederick City We are in General Sturgis's Division. Near us are the Sixty-third Indiana, the Fifty-ninth and Seventy-first New York, a Pennsylvania regiment, the Eleventh and Seventeenth Regulars, the Ninth Rhode Island regiment, and the Tenth Rhode Island battery We have devotional services every night. Quartermaster George Lewis Cooke is occupying the only meeting-house of the village for our stores, but we hear that it is to be cleared out for the chaplain the com-ing Sabbath. Last Sunday, as he had not arrived at camp, some of us got permission to go swimming, (not *fishing*,) in Rock Creek, near by We kept together, as the neighborhood is said to abound with Secesh. Close at hand was a grave-yard where several members of Union regiments were buried, who, report says, were shot while on picket duty. The picket guard fell to our company that very night, and I was glad I was not chosen, *partly* on account of the lively thunder shower we had. Last night a fellow was brought in from the picket line who had stayed out too late, we believe, courting some fair F. F V At any rate, he had on light vest and pants, and came galloping along on horseback, when Fiske, one of our mess, jumped into the middle of the road, with bayonet at the charge, and yelled, 'Who goes there?' The rider jumped back in his stirrups and pulled up, badly frightened, exclaiming, 'It's m-m-me!' 'Advance *me* and give the countersign!' 'Twas no go, he had to give it up. 'Then you're my prisoner,' says Fiske, and he had to go into camp with us for the rest of the night. 'Twas pretty rough, I'll admit, but I guess he'll keep better hours in future."

June 10th. "I was handed your letter yesterday while washing the mess pans and cups. Two are detailed for this duty each day There's no fun in it. I never realized before how much easier it is to *eat* a good dinner, than to wash the dishes afterwards. We have now been sworn into the service of the United States. There could be no 'special service at Washington' put into it, or any conditional oath whatever, and we had the choice of taking it straight, or taking a free pass home. After the oath was administered by Adjutant-General Thomas, the customary 'three cheers for your flag, men,' were heartily given. We have the best captain in the regiment, and the right of the line. One of the hardest things I have found to do yet, is to get up early enough in the morning. Reveillé comes at half-past four ! But Captain Dyer meant to wake us up the other day, and started us off as soon as we were in line, on the double-quick. Now this is all very pretty, with a company of wide-awake soldiers on a level road, but a crowd of sleepy, drowsy, raw recruits, is very different material. We had not gone far, when unfortunate number one stumbled and fell. Then graceful John Reynolds, of our mess, followed, and in the vain attempt to leap over the back of number one, was rolled into a hollow by the roadside. Then number three displayed his soles, or 'whangs,' to the rising sun, and so the fun went on, till order was finally restored, and we reached camp, as smiling and wide-awake a company as Rhode Island could produce.

"Joshua Addeman, of the college mess, has just left for home to deliver the class oration at Brown. Some of us would like to come and deliver a few at the High School, and make you a visit at the same time."

A letter to the writer, from home, dated June 14th, says: "It was college exhibition, (class day,) Thursday, and the orator was a student named Addeman, who went out in your regiment. He got a leave of absence to come on and deliver his oration, and then went back the same night. His subject was 'The Alliance of Scholarship and Patriotism.' The audience cheered him like fun, I can tell you. But he looked kind o' gray, as though he was smelling 'salt horse' in the distance!"

June 12th. "Last night was my first experience

'on picket.' Our squad marched down a lonesome-
looking road, about a mile and a half toward Fred-
ericktown, and attempted to force an entrance into
an old school-house by the roadside, but its barred
shutters resisted all our efforts. We never felt so
sorry at a school lock-out before! We marched further on, and took the best quarters we could get, in
a wheelwright shop, opening to the road. I was on
'the relief,' and had just got fairly into an uncomforta-
ble snooze, when we were all suddenly startled by
an alarm, and orders from the sergeant to buckle on
equipments, right shoulder arms, and double-quick
down the road for the picket line—all the work of
perhaps two or three minutes. Were we wide
awake? Oh, yes, some, if not some scared! But
the trouble was soon explained. Some drunken soldiers from a neighboring regiment, were attempting
to pass our line without the countersign. Order
was soon restored, and we were glad to march back to
quarters, with all the arms and legs we brought out.
It must have been about four o'clock in the morning,
when I found myself posted as sentinel. I paced
my beat, regularly, back and forth, *nothing* escaping

my keen vision. Suddenly there came the sound of approaching wheels; when, at the proper moment, with bayonet at the charge, and summoning all my voice to command, I called a 'Halt!' The occupant of the team proved to he an inoffensive fishmonger, on his way to Georgetown. He strongly protested, —and his fish still more *strongly* protested, against being interfered with—but with the help of a comrade, I marched fish and fisherman into camp, accompanied by about as tall swearing as I ever listened to. The fact is, the neighborhood around here is considered unfriendly, and it is therefore necessary to strictly maintain our lines.

June 13th. "When a box from home arrives at camp, the eatable portion of the contents, if sent to a High School boy, is considered the common property of the mess. When my box was opened, therefore, the boys all gathered round me, and as each package was taken out, they set up a terrible yelling and howling; whether they knew what was in it or not. You can guess the peanuts disappeared in double-quick time, and when I came to the lemons, there was 'tremendous applause and cheering in the 'galleries!' We not only had lots of fun over the box, but it was worth almost its weight in gold, for it contained everything I wanted. The combined knife, fork and spoon will be very useful, and will allow my fingers to take a rest, as no army knives and forks have yet been issued. The towels, also, are just what I needed, as I've been trying to make that same poor, single towel go, for more than a fortnight! You ought to have seen me skinning my fingers trying to wash it! But relief has come at last, and the contrabands now come round regularly for any washing on hand. So I 'put mine out,' to the tune of six cents apiece for shirts, and so on. I never ate any ham which tasted so good as that in the box; and we should have had small pieces if the whole High School mess had had it for dinner, for some of them are 'great feeders.' So it was agreed, that as quite a squad was going to the Potomac for a swim, those who stayed at camp should have the ham; and I tell you we enjoyed it, to the last hitch!"

June 15th. "We have a promising addition to our mess, in the form of a young contraband, thirteen years old, who boasts the name of Abraham Douglass. He has a nice voice, too, and has agreed to do our singing, and wash the dishes besides, for two dollars and fifty cents a month! Cheap enough, isn't it? The boys enjoy the singing very much, and call little Abe out every night. One of his best songs is:

· De gospel ship's a sailin'—sailin'—sailin'—
De gospel ship's a sailin'—bound for Canin's happy sho'!
CHORUS.—Then glory, glory hallelujah, &c.'

and another is:

' Dere's a light in der winder fer thee, brudder,
Dere's a light in der winder fer thee!'

"One of our men wrote home: 'The boys have found a remedy for poor rations, in songs, which carry the mind back to the scenes of other days. Within reach of the battery's guns, you may hear, rising on the air of evening, 'Jesus, lover of my soul,' or grand old Pleyel's Hymn! Here a band of students revive the memories of Brown with 'Lauriger Horatius,' 'Here's to good old Prex., drink him down!' or, 'We'll all go over to Seekonk!' while from the

other end of the camp, from the tents of the Ninth
regiment, come the strains of 'Let me kiss him for
his mother.'"

In looking over my little red-covered soldier's
hymn book, presented to the members of the Tenth
regiment, I find the following beautiful lines of "The
Countersign," pasted on the inside of the front cover
They were written by a private in Stuart's engineer
regiment, and made a deep impression on my mind:

"Halt! who goes there?" my challenge cry,
  It rings along the watchful line;
"Relief!" I hear a voice reply—
  "Advance, and give the countersign!"
With bayonet at the charge, I wait—
  The corporal gives the mystic spell—
With arms aport, I charge my mate:
  "Then onward pass, and all is well!"

But in the tent that night awake,
  I ask, if in the fray I fall,
Can I the mystic answer make
  When th' angelic sentries call?
And pray that heaven may so ordain,
  Where'er I go, what fate be mine,
Whether in travail or in pain
  I still may have "the countersign!"

"A few members of each company are allowed, now and then, a pass to Washington. The other day, a party from Company B were sauntering down Pennsylvania avenue, when a door opened across the street, and there stood General Burnside! They all ran across, with one accord, to shake hands with him, on the score of being Rhode Island soldiers. The General extended a cordial greeting to all, and inquired where the regiment was stationed; and the boys left him, feeling that this meeting alone, had amply repaid them for their tramp to Washington."

A few months later, after the battle of Antietam, young Adjutant William Ide Brown, a student of Brown University, (afterwards mortally wounded before Richmond,) thus wrote home of Burnside: "O, how I love that General! I would think myself happy if I could be an orderly, and follow him from place to place. How I wish I knew him personally! How proud I was to have him speak to me on the night of the battle of Antietam, where I was on duty at the famous Antietam bridge! There may be greater generals than Burnside, but nowhere a more honest, noble, patriotic hero!"

3

Camp Frieze, June 18th. " Yesterday afternoon, Company B was thrown into quite a flutter of excitement, by the announcement that it had been detailed for a secret expedition, and was under marching orders. We left camp at two o'clock, p. m., accompanied by the regimental officers, with directions to observe the strictest silence on the way What was going to happen? Had old Stonewall Jackson or Jeff. Davis ventured within our lines, and were the High School boys of Company B to have the glory of the capture?" Unhappily it proved not, though Stonewall *did* make a visit to Maryland a few months later, and his progress, and that of the entire rebel army, was arrested only at the terrific pass of Antietam, but sixty miles from camp. "After Company B had been marched perhaps two miles, it was halted, and faced, as the boys say, 'eyes right and left,' before a peaceful and unpretending mansion, and awaited an answer to the summons of Colonel Bliss at the front door. It seems that intelligence had reached camp that a rebel cannon was concealed on the premises, (a noted rendezvous for rebel sympathizers,) and it was con-

sidered not improbable that they might turn it to
their advantage some dark night, on our sleeping regiment at Camp Frieze. It was altogether a very serious
piece of business, the boys thought, on hearing the
news, and visions of thirty-two, if not forty-two,
pounders rose before us. The summons for surrender, however, was met by an indignant refusal from
the fair matron who answered the call, which was
warmly seconded by the old farmer himself, who
now appeared from a neighboring field. He had
been observed by some of us to be making off, but
was induced to return, after a short chase by Adjutant Tobey And now a daughter appeared on the
scene, fresh from school, and a true 'gray,' and no
mistake. She loudly declared that they would *never*
give it up. No, never! But the choice being now
given to surrender it, or take up a family march back
to camp, to the tune of ' we won't go home till morning,' they concluded to produce the gun. And lo,
what a disappointment! Instead of a mighty forty-
two pounder, or Stonewall Jackson, we beheld a small
field howitzer, such as is used in the field by infantry, and carrying a two-inch rifled ball, with effect, per-

haps a distance of two miles. But such as it was, it was mounted on its carriage and trailed back to camp by Company B, who thus earned the honor of capturing the *only* rebel cannon taken by the Tenth regiment, Rhode Island volunteers!" It is now in the possession of Rodman Post, G A. R., in Providence.

June 27th. Seminary Hill, Fairfax County, Virginia. "As per orders, we broke up our old camp shortly after midnight, yesterday morning. It was a grand sight, as the beautiful grove, with its stately oaks and tented avenues, was suddenly illuminated with huge fires, as if by magic. The long rows of glistening bayonets shone up and down the camp. The sparks filled the air and shot upward to the sky. And the scene, with the men hurrying to and fro, shouting and laughing; the falling tents, and the rumble of wagons moving off with stores and baggage, was one not soon to be forgotten. As for the High School boys, they were everywhere present, superintending everything, asking questions, and in every way helping on the excitement. By ten o'clock the regiment was in Washington, and, passing over Long Bridge, was soon on Virginia soil.

"The day was oppressively hot, but we tramped on to Alexandria, and thence to this place. Our section kept together to the end of the march, but I was so completely used up on reaching camp, that after getting a refreshing drink of water at Fort Ward, near by, I dropped *on* my rubber blanket and dropped *off* to sleep in less than two minutes. One of the boys wrote home that the length of this march had been variously estimated, according to the length of limb and strength of muscle employed, ranging from eighteen miles (about the actual distance) to thirty, and even forty; while Corporal Stump declared that he must have marched, at least, a hundred and fifty miles! Somebody innocently asked the Corporal on the way, what regiment it was, and he promptly responded ' the one hundred and tenth Rhode Island!' After the long tramp and short rest, we had to pitch our tents, the same night, on what appeared to be a vast ash-heap; to distinguish it from Camp Frieze it has been designated Camp Scorch. There is no shade whatever. The plain, as well as the surrounding hill-tops, have all been cleared of foliage and crowned with the inevitable fort. The country has been even stripped of its fences and hedges to remove every cover for the enemy. Everything has a grim, ravaged look, as far as you can see. Our regiment now forms part of a division of the reserve army corps, south of the Potomac. Corporal Nathan Baker went out on a little foraging expedition yesterday afternoon, and calling me out, on his return, displayed a single, solitary gaunt-looking chicken. It was safely landed in the High School tent, and in due time Corporal William Vaughan undertook to construct a chicken stew for the whole mess. He said he could do it, and he had never failed us on good coffee; but it proved to be 'foul play' in this case. He proceeded to fill one of our large iron mess buckets with water, prepared and placed the chicken therein; for seasoning, he used up about all our stock of pepper and salt; and after so many minutes by the watch, and a *pretended* tasting, pronounced dinner ready So we all fell in, and each had his share, as he thought, *unduly* seasoned; for each immediately passed his cup along to the next victim, with a wry face. There was plenty of stew for all, and some left for the college boys. Our cook says, 'next time draw a little *less* water, and *more* chicken!'"

Fort Pennsylvania, July 1st. "It seems the Tenth Rhode Island was not destined to long remain at Camp Scorch, in Virginia, or to further continue its march to the front. On Monday, June 30th, orders came assigning it to garrison duty in the seven forts and three batteries, protecting the capitol on the northwest; and relieving the Fifty-ninth New York Artillery, ordered to the Peninsula to join McClellan. Accordingly, on Monday, the 30th, our faces were turned back towards Alexandria, from whence we embarked for Washington, arriving a little after sunset. At half-past ten, P. M., the regiment took up its night march for Fort Pennsylvania, six miles away, near our old camp, arriving at about two o'clock, A. M. As the tents could not be unloaded from the vessel till daylight, the regiment was obliged to bivouac near the fort, without cover Fortunately, I was in a detail of men left at Washington with the baggage and stores at the vessel. Sleep, however, was difficult among the boxes, and barrels, and smells, in the hold of the schooner. After everything was put ashore, next day, two of us started for camp in charge of a provision wagon, which we

took full possession of, and were fools enough to
stuff ourselves with the Bologna sausages, greasy
cookies and pies, with which it was burdened—and
which burdened us, also, after getting to camp, with
severe headaches and loathing for sutlers' pies and
sweetmeats. But we are all right again, now. You
must remember we were *very* hungry The regiment has been distributed as follows : Companies B
and K, Captains Dyer and Low, Fort Pennsylvania, regimental headquarters ; Company D, Captain
Smith, Fort DeRussey ; Company A, Captain Taber,
Fort Franklin ; Companies E and I, Captains Cady
and Hale, Fort Alexander ; Company H, Captain
Duckworth, Batteries Vermont and Martin Scott ;
Company C, Captain Vose, Fort Cameron ; Company F, Captain Harris, Fort Ripley ; Company G,
Captain A. Crawford Greene, Fort Gaines."

Washington, July 3, 1862. Headquarters Army
of Virginia. "Don't be startled because I've turned
up in another new locality   Yesterday, while sitting
in my tent, I was summoned to officers' quarters,
and informed that Charles Wildman, of Company D,
and myself, were to be detached on special service,

at army headquarters in Washington. It seems that General Pope, from the West, has been appointed Commander of the Army of Northern Virginia, which is to include the forces of Fremont, Banks, Sturgis, and McDowell taken from McClellan. Clerks and orderlies are needed at the new headquarters, and are being detailed from the regiments around here. So, after bidding the boys good-bye, we left camp yesterday afternoon for Washington, in an ambulance wagon, with orders to report to Colonel George D. Ruggles, Chief of Staff at the War Department. We arrived there in a drenching rain, about four o'clock, but it being past business hours we were obliged to go twice, to hunt up Colonel Ruggles at his residence. We finally received an order on General Wadsworth, who referred us to the Superintendent of the Soldiers' Retreat, fully two miles away, and no umbrellas furnished, either. Remembering our hard experience at the Retreat, we concluded to retreat to the War Department, where the janitor, an Irishman, very obligingly offered us a night's lodging, which we were glad to accept, you'd better believe ! After a good square meal (just for a change) at a restaurant near by, we had the pleasure on returning, of seeing, for the first time, President Lincoln himself, in company with Senator Sumner   While sitting in the corridor, in the evening, we saw also Mr. Welles, Secretary of the Navy, with his long, white beard. Meanwhile our friend, the night-porter, had obtained permission for us to pass the night in Adjutant-General Thomas's office, which we agreed was splendid luck. So that I can report that I slept soundly last night, in the office of Uncle Sam's adjutant-general, which is more than every boy of seventeen can say   We are now at Headquarters No. 232, G street, in good health and spirits.   We think we shall like our duties first-rate.   It is a good place to see the leading military men.   General Sturgis, commanding the District troops, and General N P Banks, called to-day.   General Pope was also at the office in citizen's dress.   We are to sleep at headquarters to receive night dispatches, and take our meals close by   To-morrow is the Fourth of July   How I would enjoy spending it at home!   But here we are till the last of August.   As there will be no public celebration here, we will have a chance to look about Washington, and are promised passes from General Pope which will give us 'the freedom of the city ' Quite a privilege for high privates, we think."

July 6th. "Copied to day, from the original, a long letter from General Pope to McClellan, at Harrison's Landing, which concludes by saying that he will be ready to co-operate, in every possible way, with any future movements of the Army of the Potomac. Also a dispatch to General Banks, stating 'that the critical condition of affairs near Richmond, renders it highly probable that the rebels will advance on Washington in force.'"

July 15th. "General Pope is making arrangements to take the field. I copied, yesterday, from the original, for the government printing office, an important address to the army, of which I enclose an official copy Colonel Ruggles, Chief of Staff, read it at the office this morning, and it was pronounced just about right."

NOTE.—In view of the notoriety which this proclamation has attained, on account of General Pope's subsequent disasters, together with its admirable qualities for High School declamation, it is printed in full on the following page.

GENERAL POPE'S PROCLAMATION

"HEADQUARTERS ARMY OF VIRGINIA,

WASHINGTON, D. C., July 14, 1862.

"TO THE OFFICERS AND SOLDIERS OF THE ARMY OF VIRGINIA:

"By special assignment of the President of the United States, I have as-
sumed the command of this army. I have spent two weeks in learning your
whereabouts, your condition, and your wants; in preparing you for active ope-
rations, and in placing you in positions from which you can act promptly and
to the purpose. These labors are nearly completed, and I am about to join you
in the field.

"Let us understand each other. I have come to you from the West, where
we have always seen the backs of our enemies; from an army whose business
it has been to seek the adversary and to beat him when he was found; whose
policy has been attack and not defence. In but one instance has the enemy
been able to place our western armies in defensive attitude. I presume that I
have been called here to pursue the same system, and to lead you against the
enemy. It is my purpose to do so, and that speedily. I am sure you long for
an opportunity to win the distinction you are capable of achieving. That opportunity I shall endeavor to give you. Meantime I desire you to dismiss from
your minds certain phrases which I am sorry to find much in vogue amongst
you. I hear constantly of taking 'strong positions and holding them,' of
'lines of retreat,' and of 'bases of supplies.' Let us discard such ideas.
The strongest position a soldier should desire to occupy is one from which he
can most easily advance against the enemy. Let us study the probable lines of
retreat of our opponents, and leave our own to take care of themselves. Let
us look before us, and not behind. Success and glory are in the advance; disaster and shame lurk in the rear. Let us act on this understanding, and it is
safe to predict that your banners shall be inscribed with many a glorious deed,
and that your names will be dear to your countrymen forever.

JNO. POPE, *Major-General Commanding.*"

July 19th, Saturday. "We expect to leave Washington for the front, next Tuesday or Wednesday. The longer we remain, the smaller our chance of going with headquarters, if we return with the regiment, as our time expires in about five weeks. Have been out on horseback to Fort Pennsylvania to see the boys. Their time seems to be pretty well used up between learning heavy artillery drill, garrisoning old forts and building new ones. They were all glad to see me. They had received a box from the Ellsworth Phalanx, Captain D. W Lyman, filled with good things, which was greatly appreciated." "Wildman and I have been called out, by General Pope, on the charge of appropriating his fancy cigars! We finally got in a successful rejoinder by proving that we didn't smoke. Pope is very violent and profane, at times. This was one of the times! Now, General Sturgis was the cigar-forager We have seen him walk in and take a handful at a time; but we thought that was *his* business."

July 23, Wednesday, 9 P. M. "'All quiet on the Potomac!' I have had my bunk in the back room, on top of an old shoe-case. I rolled off, last night,

4

and jumped up, thinking we were attacked! But we
found it was only a little change of *base*, and that we
were still in Washington. Colonel Ruggles says
that arrangements to leave, cannot be completed before Friday, 25th instant. General Burnside called
the other day Also saw Hon. William H. Seward,
Secretary of State. General Pope is becoming vexed
and impatient at the continued delays. His letters
and dispatches are harder than ever to make out.
One to President Lincoln, the other day, said : 'I
am becoming anxious and uneasy to join my command in the field.' His reputation for braggadocio
is well illustrated by the following Western story :
A sick and wounded soldier was carried to the residence of General Fisk, in St. Louis, after the battle
and rebel evacuation of Corinth, where General Pope
reported he had taken ten thousand prisoners. On
a Sunday afternoon General Fisk was reading to the
wounded soldier, from First Samuel, thirtieth chap-
ter, an account of the first contraband. He was the
servant of an Amalekite, who came into David's
camp, and proposed, if assured of freedom, to show
the King of Israel a route which would enable him

to surprise his foe. The promise was given, and the King fell upon the enemy, whom he utterly destroyed. While the host was reading the list of the spoils—the prisoners, slaves, women, flocks and herds, captured by King David, the sick man looked up, and in his weak voice, piped out: 'Stop, General; just look down to the bottom of that list, and see if it isn't signed, John Pope, Major-General Commanding!' But so far as I can judge, he is the right man in the right place. There will be lively times when he takes the field. Four prisoners of the rebel cavalry were at headquarters, yesterday, for examination. They were a rough-looking set— none dressed alike. The stuff they wore, looked just like that old bagging up in the attic. Were they scared? Not any, I can tell you; neither would they give any information, but wanted to know how soon they could be exchanged, as they would like to get right back into the rebel army One of them, an adjutant of the First Virginia Cavalry, said to us, 'it will take the North a *right long* while to whip the South.' It *isn't* so easy a job as it looked to be. It don't look much like getting to Richmond at present."

July 30th. Headquarters Army of Virginia, in the Field, Warrenton, Va. "We arrived here yesterday afternoon. I was hardly fit to come, on account of a severe attack of malaria, with typhoid tendency at one time. But I was in good hands. The headquarters surgeon looked after my case, and I was very kindly cared for by a lady, who said I reminded her of an absent brother—a fortunate thing for me, wasn't it? But when I found that headquarters were really off, I insisted on going, also. So, here I am, in Warrenton, right side up, I guess, only a little the worse for wear. It took us about two hours to get here, *via* Alexandria, Manassas and Catlett's Station. The road was very rough, and the cars very rickety. Headquarters are established at the Young Ladies' Seminary, a large brick building, pleasantly located. Our office is in the main school-room, and we now occupy the school desks. I hardly expected to attend school 'down in old Virginny!' As everything here is contraband of war, we went through the desks this morning, in search of information for General Pope, and I am sorry to have to report, from the correspondence captured, that the young ladies who attend school here are very rebellious. The letters were all written like the inclosed, on coarse brown wrapping-paper. I'm inclined to think they suspected whose hands they would fall into, for one, after enlarging on her music lessons and a recent serenade, says she hopes the Yankees won't get her letters! while another, to 'My Dear Eloise,' is still more pathetic. She says : 'That was a *very* sad accident, was it not, which happened to our beloved General Ashby? It does seem as though all our distinguished men were being taken! Oh! if we could only have *piece* once more! how delightful it would be!' A letter captured by my comrade Wildman, was signed, Hattie P. Beauregard, Corinth, Miss." The Rebel prints contained notes like the following, which show the spirit of Southern women : " Messrs. Editors,—I see that General Beauregard has called for bells to be manufactured into cannon. Cannot the ladies assist by sending all their bell-metal preserving-kettles? I send mine, as a beginning.—A Southern Woman." One other : "Gentlemen,—I send you the lead weight which was attached to the striking part of our clock, with the hope that every woman in the whole confederacy will do likewise." "Great

bodies of our troops are constantly passing through
here for Culpepper. The roads are all blocked with
them. The people here are unfriendly, and openly
express their disloyal sentiments. They would like
to hang Pope."

But the poor state of my health now demanded
serious attention. Not having entirely recovered
from a fever, on leaving Washington, hard travel-
ling, hard work at my desk, and unsuitable food for
one in my condition, soon brought about a change
for the worse. So that, when headquarters were
further moved forward, August 2d, on recommenda-
tion of the surgeon, I was ordered back to Washington by Colonel Ruggles, for proper care. It was a bit-
ter disappointment, I remember, to be left behind, and
witness the gay departure of officers and comrades,
as they rode rapidly away towards Sperryville ; but
subsequent events proved it to be a kind Providence
which interposed in my behalf. From that day General Pope's headquarters were chiefly in the saddle.
Three weeks later, August 23d, they were back at
Catlett's Station, only thirty-five miles from Washington, where a midnight dash was made upon them

by the rebel cavalry; and the week following, or on the 2d of September, after fifteen days of fighting and retreating, the broken remnants of the once proud armies of Virginia were back within the defences of Washington.

August 2d, the day that the writer left General Pope's headquarters at Warrenton, my comrade Wildman wrote me, in the evening, from Sperryville : " We are encamped in a splendid place in the woods ; have wall tents, and only three in a tent. We shall fare well, as we are to have a colored cook from the cavalry. By the order just issued, we expect to come in contact with old Stonewall Jackson pretty soon." Again, on the 9th, writing from Culpepper, he says : " We arrived here yesterday. We went about a mile from the town, and opened headquarters at a large house on a farm. Of course you remember General Pope's address : ' We, in the West, have always seen the *backs* of our enemies ! Let us look before, and not behind us ! No modes of retreat,' etc. But I notice that *we* retreated last night, on the double-quick, without stopping to look behind us ! Old Stonewall was within three and a half miles of head-

quarters yesterday, and I tell you we just pulled up
stakes and travelled for Culpepper a humming. We
went way beyond the town, and had just got things
into shape, and tents up, when troop after troop of
cavalry came down the road pell-mell, till in a few
minutes it was completely blocked with them. Come
to find out, Jackson had crossed the Rapidan in force,
and driven in our pickets, and we, having cavalry
only, and he plenty of artillery, we were obliged to
retire in a hurry On the way back, we met the
brigades going out. They appeared full of fight,
and some were singing and laughing. There are between twenty and thirty thousand of our troops."

August 16th, from headquarters near Cedar Mountain, he wrote :—"On Saturday afternoon, the 9th,
the ball opened here. It was a terrific encounter.
General Banks bravely held his ground against a
vastly superior force of the rebels. Our loss was
over fifteen hundred, killed, wounded and missing.
General Pope and staff arrived on the field about
seven, P. M. They would not let the clerks go, but
I went out in the evening with the surgeons. I shall
never forget that night. There were hundreds and

hundreds of wounded. The battle was over, but an
artillery fire was kept up till midnight. I went out
again on Tuesday last, 12th instant, and saw the old
devils, just as the last of them skedaddled for the
Rapidan. I came near getting my old head knocked
off, too. I tell you that was quite a little fight.
Colonel Ruggles had a horse shot under him. Colonel Morgan, who signed your last pass, got a bullet
through his hat, and, in fact, Pope and the whole
staff came near being captured. We move again to-
morrow, to the Rapidan. We now have a colored
cook, and have ordered cooking utensils forwarded
from Washington." But on that very day, the 16th
of August, a party of rebel cavalry was captured
near by, informing General Pope, through an auto-
graph letter of General Lee's, that the latter was
moving northward, by forced marches, with the entire rebel army of Richmond, to attack him. In
consequence of this information, General Pope has-
tily broke up his camps on the Rapidan and retired to
a position behind the north branch of the Rappahan-
nock, in the hope that by holding the fords, sufficient time would be gained for the Army of the Poto-

mac to reinforce him. Unhappily this result utterly
failed. On Friday evening, August 22d, General
Pope's train and headquarters were back at Catlett's
Station, within thirty-five miles of Washington, where
a night attack was made by a body of Stonewall
Jackson's cavalry, under General Stuart. It was a
complete surprise, and met with only slight resist-
ance. My comrade Wildman, of the Tenth regiment, who was there, said that they were betrayed
by a contraband who had been supplied with food
the day before. Thus guided, the rebels moved
silently forward to the very tents of Pope's officers,
and poured in a deadly volley Some were killed on
both sides. In the darkness and confusion which
followed, many escaped; but the raiders captured
over two hundred prisoners, a still greater number
of the General's horses, his personal baggage, including his uniform, and everything belonging to his
staff officers. One of the staff was captured, and
also one of the clerks. As for my friend Wildman,
he was only too glad to get off alive. But he had a
rough time, and a hard tramp through the mud, rain
and darkness, to reach a place of safety The raid-

ers retired to Warrenton, Pope's headquarters only three weeks before, and were received with ovations by the people. The bells were rung, a procession formed, and a contraband, arrayed in General Pope's uniform, was paraded on horseback through the streets.

At the time of the departure of the Tenth Rhode Island for home, a few days after, August 25th, it was believed that the armies of Generals Pope and McClellan had safely effected a junction near Manassas; that the emergency had passed, and that the united armies of Virginia would soon be in a position to resume the offensive. The regiment's term of service had not only expired, but not less than seventy-five of the men, including Colonel Bliss, had left to join the new Seventh regiment. Others were to receive commissions, or would re-enlist in the new colored battalion being recruited at Providence. My comrade Wildman rejoined the regiment on its homeward journey, at Washington, and as he told the story of his adventures and escape, in the night attack on Pope's headquarters, he was the centre of interest. He thought the clerks' order "for cooking "utensils, at Cedar Mountain," might safely be countermanded, and was willing to let General Pope's "lines of retreat" "take care of themselves!"

The Tenth regiment arrived home on the steamer Bay State, from Elizabethport, N. J., on the morning of the 28th of August. It was received with a national salute, and escorted to Exchange Place, where it was dismissed to the various armories. Company B was entertained in the Fourth Ward drill-room in the Calender building, with generous hospitality The students especially appreciated the words of welcome from President Sears, of Brown University. The High School boys were afterward given a rousing reception by the Ellsworth Phalanx, Captain Lyman, in High School hall, where, if the writer remembers, there were some rude attempts at oratory On Sunday evening, August 31st, the regiment attended divine service at the Beneficent Congregational church, where interesting addresses were delivered by our chaplain, the pastor of the church, Rev Mr Clapp; Dr. Hitchcock, and others. On Monday, September 1st, 1862, the regiment was mustered out of service, and its military record closed.

Of the students of Company B, Captain Elisha Dyer afterwards wrote : "They proved themselves worthy of the sacred cause for which they enlisted. For no delinquency or misdemeanor did any name of theirs ever find a place on the morning report. Always prompt, obedient and efficient, they won for themselves an honorable record."

And in his final report to the Governor, Colonel Shaw says : "The character and conduct of the men were all that could be desired. The guard house was almost a useless institution. We were permitted to perform but an humble part in the great struggle for all that we hold most dear ; but I hope that that part was well done, and that it will meet your approval, and the approval of the citizens of our honored State."

[Read before the Society, February 14, 1882.]

In Memoriam

ROLL OF STUDENTS OF THE PROVIDENCE HIGH SCHOOL

WHO

LOST THEIR LIVES IN THE SERVICE OF THEIR COUNTRY DURING THE REBELLION.

NOTE. The year given is, in all cases, that of *entering* the school.

MUNROE H. GLADDING,	Class of 1843.
FRANCIS B. FERRIS,	" 1845.
WILLIAM WARE HALL,	" 1845.
JOHN P. SHAW,	" 1847.
GEORGE W. FIELD,	" 1849.
JAMES H. EARLE,	" 1850.
HOWARD GREENE,	" 1852.
GEORGE WHEATON COLE,	" 1853.
SAMUEL FOSTER, 2D,	" 1853.
JESSE COMSTOCK,	" 1855.
J. NELSON BOGMAN,	" 1858.
PETER HUNT,	" 1858.
WILLIAM F. ATWOOD,	" 1859.
BENJAMIN E. KELLY,	" 1859.
CHARLES M. LATHAM,	" 1859.
FREDERICK METCALF,	" 1861.
EUGENE F. GRANGER.	" 1863.

ROLL OF TEACHERS AND STUDENTS

OF THE PROVIDENCE HIGH SCHOOL WHO SERVED IN THE ARMY
OR NAVY OF THE UNITED STATES DURING THE REBELLION.

———————◆———————

NOTE. The year given is, in all cases, that of *entering* the school.

TEACHERS.

EDWARD H. HALL, (of Class of 1843, and Assistant
Teacher, 1854)
   Chaplain 44th Massachusetts Volunteers.

WILLIAM A. MOWRY, (Teacher English Dep't. 1858–1864).
   Captain Company K, 11th Rhode Island Volunteers, October
   1, 1862—July 13, 1863.

SAMUEL THURBER, (of Class of 1849, and Teacher Junior
and Classical Departments, 1859–1865)
   Private Company I, 11th Rhode Island Volunteers, October
   1, 1862; Second Lieutenant Company K, November 3; First
   Lieutenant March 26,—July 13, 1863.

JOHN J. LADD, (Teacher Classical Dep't. 1859–1864).
   Paymaster, with rank of Major, Ohio Volunteers.

ALPHONSE RENAUD, (Teacher of French, 1860–1864).
   Sergeant Troop G, 3d Rhode Island Cavalry, March 14, 1864—
   November 29, 1865.

ALONZO WILLIAMS, (Assistant Teacher, 1869–1870).
   Private Company A, Third Rhode Island Heavy Artillery,
   September 6, 1861; Corporal, June 1, 1862; Sergeant, January
   1, 1863; Quartermaster-Sergeant and First Sergeant Battery
   A, 3d Rhode Island Heavy Artillery, 1864; Second Lieuten-
   ant, July 6, 1865. On detached service in 1863, as gunner in
   United States Navy. Mustered out August 4, 1865.

STUDENTS.

ENTERED IN CLASS OF 1843.

EDWARD ABORN,

Private Company D, 1st Rhode Island Volunteers, May 30,—
August 2, 1861. Private Company D, 10th Rhode Island
Volunteers, May 26,—September 1, 1862. Second Lieutenant
Company D, 14th Rhode Island Heavy Artillery, (colored,)
September 28, 1863. Resigned January 22, 1865.

JAMES H. ARMINGTON,

Second Lieutenant Company D, and Quartermaster, 10th
Rhode Island Volunteers, May 26,—September 1, 1862.

MARTIN P. BUFFUM,

Private Company C, 1st Rhode Island Volunteers, May 2,
1861. Discharged May 31, for disability. First Lieuten-
ant, September 17, and Captain Company B, 4th Rhode Island
Volunteers, October 30, 1861. Major, October 4, 1862. Lieuten-
ant-Colonel, December 24, 1862. Taken prisoner July 30,
1864, in attack on fortifications before Petersburg; released
December 8, 1864; mustered out December 17, 1864. Brevet
Colonel March 13, 1865. Lieutenant-Colonel 9th Veteran
Regiment 1st Army Corps, June 1, 1865. Second and First
Lieutenant and Captain 15th United States Infantry, 1866.
Since resigned.

WILLIAM S. CHACE,

Second Lieutenant Company E, 4th Regiment, Rhode Island
Volunteers, October 30, 1861. Captain, November 20, 1861.
Severely wounded, March 14, 1862, at the battle of Newbern,
N. C. Resigned July 18, 1862. First Lieutenant Hospital
Guards, Rhode Island Volunteers, November 12, 1862—
August 26, 1865.

CHARLES H. DUNHAM,

Orderly Sergeant, Company C, 1st Rhode Island Volunteers,
May 2,—August 2, 1861. Appointed Captain Company D,
10th Rhode Island Volunteers. Resigned.

CYRUS G. DYER.

Quartermaster 1st Rhode Island Volunteers, May 2, 1861. Captain 2d Rhode Island Volunteers, June 5, 1861. Major 12th Rhode Island Volunteers, October 17, 1862. Wounded December 13, 1862, at Fredericksburg, and mustered out July 29th, 1863, Captain 26th United States Colored Troops.

MUNROE H. GLADDING,

Private Company C, 1st Rhode Island Volunteers, May 2,— August 2, 1861. Quartermaster, 5th Rhode Island Volunteers, January, 1862. On leave of absence, and died at Beaufort, S. C., October 4, 1862.

EDWARD H. HALL, (also Assistant Teacher in High School 1854)

Chaplain 44th Massachusetts Volunteers.

HENRY K. POTTER,

Corporal Company C, 1st Rhode Island Volunteers, May 2,— August 2, 1861. Sergeant Company A, 11th Rhode Island Volunteers, October 1, 1862—July 13, 1863.

JAMES SHAW, JR.,

Lieutenant-Colonel 10th Rhode Island Volunteers, May 26, 1862. Colonel, August 6 to September 1, 1862. Lieutenant-Colonel 12th Rhode Island Volunteers, December 31, 1862, to July 29, 1863. Colonel 7th United States Colored Troops, October 27, 1863. Commanding 1st Brigade, 3d Division 10th Army Corps; 1st Brigade, 2d Division 25th Army Corps. Mustered out November 16, 1866. Brevet Brigadier-General, March 13, 1865.

SAMUEL B. TOBEY,

Lieutenant and Quartermaster 3d New York Heavy Artillery.

CLASS OF 1844.

NATHAN S. K. DAVIS,

Sergeant Company K, 10th Rhode Island Volunteers, May 26, —September 1, 1862.

JOSEPH P. MANTON,

Volunteer attached to Carbineers with 1st Rhode Island Volunteers at Battle of Bull Run, July 21, 1861. Colonel and Aid-de-Camp on Staff of Governor William Sprague.

CHARLES H. MUMFORD,

First Lieutenant Company I, 10th Rhode Island Volunteers, May 26,—September 1, 1862. First Lieutenant Company C, 14th Rhode Island Heavy Artillery, (colored,) 1863. Resigned for disability, July 20, 1864.

CLASS OF 1845.

DANIEL T. A. BOWLER.

WILLIAM E. CUTTING,

Corporal Company D, 1st Rhode Island Volunteers, May 2,— August 2, 1861.

WINTHROP DEWOLF,

Private Company C, 1st Rhode Island Volunteers, June 14,— August 2, 1861. Private Company D, and Quartermaster 10th Rhode Island Volunteers, May, 1862. Captain Company D, August 1,—September 1, 1862.

FRANCIS B. FERRIS,

Captain Company I, 12th Illinois Volunteers, April 25, 1861. Mortally wounded April 6, 1862, at the battle of Shiloh, and died April 18, 1862, at Paducah, Ky.

WILLIAM WARE HALL,

First Lieutenant Company B, 5th Regiment Rhode Island Heavy Artillery, 1861. Resigned in summer of 1862. Teacher to the Freedmen in 1863 and 1864. Died of disease contracted in the service, July 1, 1864.

RICHARD G. SHAW,

Captain Company D, 3d Rhode Island Volunteers, August 27, 1861. Resigned January 13, 1864. Major, 14th Rhode Island Heavy Artillery, (colored,) January 31, 1864,—October 2, 1865. Second Lieutenant and First Lieutenant 1st United States Artillery. Now Brevet Captain United States Army.

JOHN TURNER,

Adjutant 12th Rhode Island Volunteers, October 13, 1862. Resigned December 25, 1862.

CLASS OF 1846.

JAMES ANNIS,

Private Company H, 10th Rhode Island Volunteers, May 26, —September 1, 1862.

HENRY A. DEWITT,

Private Company C, 1st Rhode Island Volunteers, May 2, 1861. Promoted to Engineer, rank of Second Lieutenant, May 31, 1861. Mustered out August 2, 1861.

ARTHUR F. DEXTER,

Captain Company A, 1st Rhode Island Volunteers, May 2,— August 2, 1861. On Staff Brigadier General Tyler, April, 1862. Resigned.

JOHN H. HAMMOND,

Sergeant Battery A, 1st Rhode Island Light Artillery, June 6, 1861. Wounded June 30, 1862, at battle before Richmond, Va. Discharged October, 1862, on Surgeon's certificate. Second Lieutenant Hospital Guards, Rhode Island Volunteers, December 13, 1862,—August 26, 1865.

CHARLES H. MERRIMAN,

Adjutant 1st Rhode Island Volunteers, May 2,—August 2, 1861. Appointed Major 10th Rhode Island Volunteers, May 26, 1862. Resigned.

FRANK WHEATON,

First Lieutenant 4th United States Cavalry, March 3, 1855. Captain U. S. Cavalry, March 1, 1861. Lieutenant-Colonel 2d

Rhode Island Volunteers, June, 1861; Colonel, July 22,
1861. Brigadier-General Volunteers, November 29, 1862.
Major 2d Cavalry, United States Army, November 5, 1863.
Brevet Colonel United States Army, October 19, 1864. Bre-
vet Major-General Volunteers, October 19, 1864. Brevet
Lieutenant-Colonel United States Army, May 5, 1864, for
bravery at the Battle of the Wilderness. Brevet Colonel,
June, 1864. Brevet Brigadier-General, April, 1865. Brevet
Major-General United States Army, July, 1865. After the
close of war, Lieutenant-Colonel 39th United States Infan-
try, November, 1865. Still in the service, Colonel 2d United
States Infantry.

CLASS OF 1847.

SYLVESTER MARBLE,

Corporal Company A, 1st Rhode Island Volunteers, May 2,—
August 2, 1861.

WILLIAM MARCHANT,

Private Company K, 1st Rhode Island Volunteers, May 2,—
August 2, 1861.

LEWIS H. METCALF,

Private Ellsworth Zouave Regiment, New York Volunteers,
April, 1861. Lost a leg and taken prisoner at Bull Run,
July 21, 1861, and carried to Richmond. Exchanged and
mustered out October, 1862, on surgeon's certificate.

JOHN P SHAW,

Sergeant-Major 1st Rhode Island Volunteers, April 18, 1861.
Second Lieutenant Company F, 2d Rhode Island Volunteers, June 6, 1861; First Lieutenant, July 22, 1861; Captain July 24, 1862. Killed at Battle of the Wilderness, May
12, 1864.

ALEXANDER V G. TAYLOR,

Private Company C, 1st Rhode Island Volunteers, May 2,—
August 2, 1861.

CLASS OF 1848.

WILLIAM E. BOWEN,

> First Sergeant Battery E, September 3'), 1861. Mustered out March 14, 1862, for disability

THOMAS H. CARRIQUE,

> Private Company M, 3d Regiment Rhode Island Heavy Artillery, January, 1862. Second Lieutenant Company H, February, 1863. First Lieutenant, February, 1864. Commissioned by War Department, First Lieutenant in Signal Corps, United States Army, August 8, 1864. Mustered out at close of war.

FRANCIS W GODDARD,

> Private Company C, 1st Rhode Island Volunteers, May 2, 1861. Captain Carbineers, June 27, 1861. Mustered out August 2, 1861.

LEVI R. GREENE,

> Third Assistant Engineer United States Navy, September, 1857. Second Assistaut Engineer, on Frigate Niagara, 1860, which conveyed Japanese Commission to Japan. Returned to United States in April, 1861. Without landing, ordered, April 17, to blockade off Charleston, S. C., and captured the first prize of the war. Served in Gulf Squadron, June, 1862. On special duty at Baltimore, 1863, and at Providence, R. I., to superintend construction government machinery. First Assistant Engineer (Master) United States Navy, October 15, 1863. Served in James River Squadron until the surrender of Richmond. Served in Brazil Squadron 1865—1866. On special service at Boston, 1867—1868. Resigned July 1, 1869.

JAMES NICHOLS,

> Sergeant Company F, 5th Rhode Island Volunteers, August 14, 1862—June 26, 1863.

SAMUEL A PEARCE, JR.,

> First Lieutenant 10th Rhode Island Battery, May 26,—August 30, 1862. Additional Paymaster United States Army; Major and Brevet Lieutenant-Colonel, 1864.

HORATIO ROGERS, JR.,

First Lieutenant 3d Rhode Island Heavy Artillery, August 27, 1861. Captain, October 9, 1861. Major, August 18, 1862. Colonel 11th Rhode Island Volunteers, December 27, 1862. Colonel 2d Rhode Island Volunteers, January 29, 1863. Resigned and mustered out January 14, 1864. Brevet Brigadier-General United States Volunteers, March 13, 1865.

CHARLES H. TOMPKINS,

Captain 1st Battery, April, 1861. Major 1st Rhode Island Light Artillery, August 1, 1861. Colonel, September 13, 1861, Chief of Artillery under Brigadier-General Stone, November, 1861, and General Sedgwick, in Virginia campaigns of 1862, 1863 and 1864. Brevet Brigadier-General, August 1, 1864. Chief of Artillery 6th Army Corps. Mustered out April 21, 1865.

CLASS OF 1849.

THEODORE ANDREWS,

Private Company D, 1st Rhode Island Volunteers, May 2,–August 2, 1861.

NICHOLAS B. BOLLES,

First Lieutenant Company H, 10th Rhode Island Volunteers, May 26,–September 1, 1862.

GEORGE E. CHURCH,

Captain Company C, 7th Rhode Island Volunteers, July 26, 1862. Lieutenant-Colonel, January 27, 1863. Colonel 11th Rhode Island Volunteers, February 28,–July 6, 1863. Appointed Colonel 2nd Rhode Island Volunteers, December 31, 1864, but not mustered.

GEORGE W FIELD,

Corporal Battery A, 1st Rhode Island Light Artillery, 1861. First Lieutenant Battery F, 1862. Resigned October 26, 1862. Second Lieutenant Company B, 4th Rhode Island Volunteers. Killed July 30, 1864, in attack on fortifications before Petersburg, Va.

WILLIAM A. HARRIS,

Private Company D, 10th Regiment Rhode Island Volunteers, May 26,–September 1, 1862.

JEFFREY HAZARD,

> Second Lieutenant Battery A. 1st Rhode Island Light Artillery, and Regimental Adjutant October 5, 1861. Captain Battery H, October 1, 1862. Resigned August 17, 1863.

JAMES S. HUDSON,

> Private Company D, 1st Rhode Island Volunteers, May 2,—August 2, 1861. First Lieutenant Company F, 11th Rhode Island Volunteers, October 1, 1862—July 13, 1863.

HAZARD A. REYNOLDS,

> Private Company K, 2d Rhode Island Volunteers, June 5, 1861. Wounded at the Battle of Bull Run, July 21, 1861. Sergeant Company K, July 22, 1861. Mustered out June 17, 1864.

FRANK A. RHODES,

> First Lieutenant 10th Rhode Island Battery, May 26,—September 1, 1862.

JACOB SILLOWAY, JR.,

> First Lieutenant 6th New York Volunteers, May 25, 1861—June 26, 1863.

SAMUEL THURBER, (also teacher in High School, 1859-'65).

> Private Company I, Second Lieutenant and First Lieutenant Company K, 11th Rhode Island Volunteers, October 1, 1862 —July 13, 1863.

JOHN A. TOMPKINS,

> Major 1st Rhode Island Light Artillery, October 1, 1862. Brevet Lieutenant-Colonel, August 1, 1864. Lieutenant-Colonel November 1, 1864. Acting Assistant Inspector of Artillery Middle Military Division. Mustered out March 29, 1865.

CLASS OF 1850.

JOHN C. BABCOCK,

> Captain and Chief of Scouts with Grant's army.

CHARLES H. BARTLETT,

Sergeant Company H, 11th Rhode Island Volunteers, October 1, 1862—July 13, 1863.

J. HALSEY DEWOLF,

Private Company D, 10th Rhode Island Volunteers, May 26,—September 1, 1862.

JAMES H. EARLE,

Assistant Paymaster United States Navy. Prisoner of war and died at Andersonville.

ROBERT H. I. GODDARD,

Private Company C, 1st Rhode Island Volunteers, May 2,—August 2, 1861. Lieutenant and volunteer Aid-de-Camp on General Burnside's staff, September 20, 1862. Captain March 11, 1863. Brevet Major, August 4, 1864. Brevet Lieutenant-Colonel April 2, 1865, and Assistant Inspector-General 9th Army Corps. Mustered out at close of the war.

GEORGE O. GORTON,

Private Company C, 1st Rhode Island Volunteers, May 2, 1861. First Sergeant Carbineers, June 27,—August 2, 1861. Second Lieutenant Company M, 3d Rhode Island Heavy Artillery, February 5, 1862. First Lieutenant Company B, October 28, and Adjutant, November 1, 1862. Appointed Captain November 2, 1863, but declined muster. Mustered out October 5, 1864.

ARNOLD GREEN,

Private Company C, First Rhode Island Volunteers, May 29, —August 2, 1861.

EARL C. HARRIS,

Second Lieutenant Company H, 1st Rhode Island Volunteers, May 2,—August 2, 1861.

JOEL METCALF, JR.,

Sergeant Company F, 10th Rhode Island Volunteers, May 26, —September 1, 1862. First Lieutenant and Captain Company H, 11th Rhode Island Volunteers, October 1, 1862—

6

July 13, 1863. Captain Company D, 14th Rhode Island
Heavy Artillery (colored), September 22, 1863—October 2,
1865.

JOSEPH H. METCALF,

Second Lieutenant, First Lieutenant and Adjutant 14th Maine
Volunteers. Captain and Assistant Adjutant-General
United States Volunteers, September 4, 1863. Mustered out
at close of war.

MUNSON H. NAJAC,

Sergeant Company A, 1st Rhode Island Volunteers, May 2,—
August 2, 1861. First Sergeant Company K, 10th Rhode
Island Volunteers, May 26,—September 1, 1862. Second
Lieutenant Company I, 12th Rhode Island Volunteers,
October 13, 1862. First Lieutenant Company I, February
19,—July 29, 1863.

CLASS OF 1851.

FRANK G. ALLEN,

Corporal 1st Rhode Island Battery, May 2,—August 6, 1861.
Appointed Quartermaster New York Cavalry, 1862, but resigned for disability. Volunteer Aid on Staff General Con-
ner, 1864.

FREDERIC S. BATCHELLER,

Private Company D, 1st Rhode Island Volunteers, May 2,—
August 2, 1861.

ALBERT G. BATES,

First Lieutenant Company G, 1st Rhode Island Volunteers,
May 2,—August 2, 1861. Sergeant Company D, 11th Rhode
Island Volunteers, October 1, 1862. Second Lieutenant
Company C, November 6, 1862. Mustered out July 13, 1863.

LEANDER C BELCHER,

Second Lieutenant Company A, 10th Rhode Island Volunteers, May 26,—September 2, 1862.

WILLIAM B. BENNETT,

Private Company C, 1st Rhode Island Volunteers, May 2,—
August 1, 1861.

Lucius S. Bolles,

Assistant Surgeon 2d Rhode Island Volunteers, March 9,—September 10, 1863.

Samuel T. Browne,

Private Company D, 10th Rhode Island Volunteers, May 26, —September 1, 1862. Volunteer Assistant Paymaster United States Navy, September 30, 1862. Served in North and South Atlantic blockading squadron till close of war. Assistant Paymaster (Master), March 9, 1865. Served in Asiatic squadron 1866—1869. Naval Storekeeper at Rio de Janeiro, 1870, and at Annapolis, Md., from 1873 to 1877. Died on United States Ship Powhattan, Newport, R. I., June 15, 1881.

John H. Cady,

Private Company D, 10th Rhode Island Volunteers, May 26, —September 1, 1862.

Francis V Kelly,

Private Troop C, 2d Rhode Island Cavalry, December 12, 1862. Transferred to 1st Louisiana Cavalry, August 24, 1863. Transferred to 3d Rhode Island Cavalry, Troop I, January 14, 1864. Mustered out at close of war.

George E. Randolph,

Sergeant-Major Battery A, 1st Rhode Island Light Artillery, June 6, 1861. Wounded July 21, 1861, at Battle of Bull Run, Virginia. Second Lieutenant August 14, 1861. First Lieutenant Battery C, September 13, 1861. Captain Battery E, September 30, 1861. Chief of Artillery 3d Army Corps, 1863—at Gettysburg. Resigned December 29, 1863. Brevet Major, Lieutenant-Colonel and Colonel, United States Volunteers.

Richard K. Randolph,

Lieutenant Company I, 12th Illinois Volunteers, 16th Army Corps, and Acting Assistant Adjutant-General, 1861. Taken prisoner at the Battle of Shiloh, April 6, 1862. Put in irons for attempting to escape. Exchanged November, 1862, and honorably discharged.

WILLIAM E. TABER, JR.,

 Private Company A, 1st Rhode Island Volunteers, May 2,—
 August 2, 1861. Captain Company A, 10th Rhode Island
 Volunteers, May 26,—September 1, 1862.

RICHARD WATERMAN.

 Private 1st Battery Rhode Island Light Artillery, May 2,—
 August 2, 1861. First Lieutenant Battery C, August 8, 1861.
 Captain Battery C, July 25, 1862—September 2, 1864.

CLASS OF 1852.

WILLIAM C. ALMY,

 Private Company A, 1st Rhode Island Volunteers, May 2,—
 August 2, 1861.

AMOS M. BOWEN,

 Private Company A, 1st Rhode Island Volunteers, Enlisted
 April 15, 1861. Captured at Battle of Bull Run, July 21, 1861.
 A prisoner at Richmond, Virginia, and Salisbury, North
 Carolina. Exchanged May 22, 1862. First Lieutenant Com-
 pany C, 2d Rhode Island Volunteers, January 22, 1863.
 Aid-de-Camp on staff of General Eustis. Mustered out
 June 17, 1864.

HOWARD GREENE,

 Lieutenant 24th Wisconsin Volunteers, at Antietam, 1862.
 Captain on General Lytle's Staff, 1863. Killed at Mission-
 ary Ridge in a charge on the enemy, November 25, 1863.

EDWARD N. GOULD,

 Corporal Company D, 10th Rhode Island Volunteers, May
 26,—September 1, 1862.

THOMAS J. GRIFFIN,

 Private Company A, and Hospital Steward, 1st Rhode Island
 Volunteers, May 2,—August 2, 1861. Hospital Steward, 4th
 Rhode Island Volunteers, October 30, 1861—October 15, 1864.

J. ALBERT MONROE,

 First Lieutenant Battery A, 1st Rhode Island Light Artillery,
 June 6, 1861. Captain Battery D, September 7, 1861. Chief

of Artillery General Doubleday's Division. Major and Lieutenant-Colonel 1st Rhode Island Light Artillery, October 21, 1862—October 5, 1864 Afterwards assigned to special duty of establishing an Artillery Camp of Instruction near Washington, D. C.

McWALTER B. NOYES,
Chaplain 5th Rhode Island Volunteers, November 7, 1861—August 15, 1862.

FRANK H. THURBER,
Private Company K, 10th Rhode Island Volunteers, May 26,—September 1, 1862.

AMASA C. TOURTELLOT,
First Sergeant 10th Battery Rhode Island Volunteers, May 26,—August 30, 1862.

WILLIAM L. WHEATON,
Hospital Steward 2d Rhode Island Volunteers, June 6, 1861. Second Lieutenant Company F, September 28, 1861. First Lieutenant Company F, July 24, 1862.

CLASS OF 1853.

WILLIAM H. AYER,
Private Company I, 10th Rhode Island Volunteers, May 26,—September 1, 1862. First Lieutenant Company A, 11th Rhode Island Volunteers, October 1, 1862. Captain Company A, December 31, 1862—July 13, 1863.

CHARLES H. BEEDLE,
Corporal Company K, 10th Rhode Island Volunteers, May 26,—September 1, 1862.

HORACE S. BRADFORD,
Acting Assistant Paymaster, United States Navy, February 24, 1862—December 1, 1863.

THOMAS T. CASWELL,
Assistant Paymaster (Master), United States Navy, September 9, 1861. Paymaster (Lieutenant-Commander), September 17, 1863. Still in the service.

GEORGE WHEATON COLE.

Master's Mate, United States Navy. 1861. Killed April 24, 1862, on Sloop of war "Iroquois," at the capture of Fort Jackson, Mississippi river.

SAMUEL T CUSHING.

Captain and Commissary Subsistence of Volunteers, United States Army, February 9, 1863.

JAMES A. DEWOLF,

Private Company C, 1st Rhode Island Volunteers, May 2,— August 2, 1861. Captain and Commissary Subsistence of Volunteers United States Army, November 16, 1861.

WILLIAM W DOUGLAS.

Second Lieutenant Company B, 5th Rhode Island Heavy Artillery, November 30, 1861. First Lieutenant Company D, June 7, 1862. Captain Company D, February 14, 1863— December 20, 1864.

CORNELIUS DRAPER,

Private Company C, 1st Rhode Island Volunteers, May 2,— August 2, 1862.

SAMUEL FOSTER, 2D,

Corporal Company D, 1st Rhode Island Volunteers, May 2, 1861. Missing and undoubtedly killed at Battle of Bull Run, Va., July 21, 1861.

WILLIAM W HOPPIN, JR.,

Private Company C, 1st Rhode Island Volunteers, May 2,— August 2, 1861.

PARDON S. JASTRAM.

Private Company C, 1st Rhode Island Volunteers, May 2,— August 2, 1861. Second Lieutenant 1st Rhode Island Light Artillery, October 16, 1861. First Lieutenant, December 6, 1862. Assistant Adjutant-General Artillery Brigade, 3d Army Corps. Resigned March 29, 1864.

GEORGE E. MASON,

Assistant Surgeon 1st Massachusetts Heavy Artillery, April 7,—August 25, 1865.

BENJAMIN F PABODIE,

Corporal Company H, 10th Rhode Island Volunteers, May 26,
—September 1, 1862.

THOMAS T. POTTER,

Private Company B, 10th Rhode Island Volunteers, May 26,
—September 1, 1862.

WILLIAM M. SILLOWAY,

Private Company C, 2d Rhode Island Volunteers, July 5, 1861.
Transferred to Veteran Reserve Corps, December 15, 1863.

HENRY K. SOUTHWICK,

Second Lieutenant Company F, 2d Rhode Island Volunteers,
August 29, 1862. First Lieutenant Company F, August 24,
1863. Captain Company M, 14th Rhode Island Heavy Artillery (colored), March 24, 1864—October 2, 1865.

HENRY J. SPOONER,

Second Lieutenant 4th Rhode Island Volunteers, August 27,
1862. First Lieutenant and Adjutant, October 1, 1862; also
Acting Adjutant 7th Rhode Island Volunteers. Mustered
out in 1865.

ROBERT H. THURSTON,

Third Assistant Engineer United States Navy (Midshipman),
July 29, 1861. Second Assistant Engineer (Ensign), December 18, 1862. First Assistant Engineer (Master), January 30, 1865. Now in the service.

BENJAMIN N. WILBUR,

Private Company B, 10th Rhode Island Volunteers, May 26,
—September 1, 1863. Also served in 61st Mass. Vols.

CLASS OF 1854.

THOMAS J. ABBOTT,

Private Company A, 1st Rhode Island Volunteers, May 2,—
August 2, 1861.

JOSHUA M. ADDEMAN,

Private Company B, 10th Rhode Island Volunteers, May 26,
—September 1, 1862. Captain Company H, 14th Rhode
Island Heavy Artillery (colored), November 23, 1863—Octo-
ber 2, 1865.

CHARLES D. CADY.

Volunteer with 1st Rhode Island Volunteers, at Battle of Bull Run, Virginia, July 21, 1861.

CHARLES II. CHAPMAN,

Adjutant 5th Rhode Island Volunteers, December 16, 1861—May 10, 1862; also served in 39th Massachusetts Volunteers. Captain 41st Regiment United States Colored Troops.

EDWIN LOWE.

Private Company D, 1st Rhode Island Volunteers, May 2, 1861. Honorably discharged June 4, 1861. Sergeant Company C, 12th Rhode Island Volunteers, October 13, 1862—July 29, 1863.

WILLIAM A. RICHARDSON,

Private Company D, 2d Rhode Island Volunteers, June 6, 1861—June 17, 1864.

CHARLES D. THURBER,

Private Company K, 10th Rhode Island Volunteers, May 26, —September 1, 1862.

CLASS OF 1855.

WILLIAM B. AVERY,

Private Company A, 1st Rhode Island Volunteers, May 2,—August 2, 1861. Master's Mate Coast Division, Burnside Expedition, December 25, 1861. Second Lieutenant New York Marine Artillery, February 15, 1862. First Lieutenant, July 1, 1862. Captain, August 1, 1862. Chief of Artillery on General Ledlie's staff, January 17, 1863. Acting Ensign United States Navy, June 15, 1863. Served as Acting Master and mustered out August 10, 1865.

JOHN T. BLAKE,

Sergeant Battery B, 1st Rhode Island Light Artillery, August 13, 1861. Wounded at Gettysburg, Pa., July 2, 1863. Second Lieutenant Battery A, October 28, 1863. Mustered out August 12, 1864.

EDWIN BOSS,

Assistant Paymaster United States Navy.

T. FRED. BROWN,

Corporal Battery A, 1st Rhode Island Light Artillery, June 6, 1861. Second Lieutenant Battery C, August 13, 1862. First Lieutenant Battery B, December 29, 1862. Wounded at Gettysburg, July 2, 1863. Captain, April 7, 1864. Brevet Major, December 3, 1864. Brevet Lieutenant-Colonel, April 9, 1865. Inspector-General Artillery Brigade, 2d Army Corps. Mustered out June 12, 1865.

FREDERICK L. BROWN,

Second Lieutenant Company H, 3d Rhode Island Heavy Artillery, January 8, 1862. Resigned July 6, 1862.

EDWARD W BROWN,

Sergeant Company D, 10th Rhode Island Volunteers, May 26, —September 1, 1862.

WILLIAM C. CHASE,

First Sergeant, Second Lieutenant and First Lieutenant Company B, 10th Rhode Island Volunteers, May 26,—September 2, 1862.

JESSE COMSTOCK,

Private Company D, 1st Rhode Island Volunteers, May 2,— August 2, 1861. Wounded and missing at Battle of Bull Run, Va., July 21, 1861. Afterwards died, aged 18 years, 5 months and 20 days.

FRANKLIN COOLEY,

Corporal Company G, 10th Rhode Island Volunteers, May 26, —September 2, 1862.

CHARLES G. KING,

Hospital Steward, 10th Rhode Island Volunteers, May 26,— September 1, 1862.

HENRY S. LATHAM, JR.,

Private Company B, 10th Rhode Island Volunteers, May 26,— September 1, 1862.

WILLIAM H. MARTIN,

> Sergeant Company C, 4th Rhode Island Volunteers, October 30, 1861. Wounded September 17, 1862, at Antietam. Discharged December 31, 1862, for disability.

ISAAC P NOYES,

> Private Battery H, 1st Rhode Island Light Artillery, October 14, 1862—June 28, 1865.

HENRY E. PAYNE,

> Assistant Surgeon United States Army,

WILLIAM J. POTTER,

> United States Navy, May, 1863—July, 1864.

ORVILLE M. REMINGTON,

> Private Company C, 1st Rhode Island Volunteers, May 2,—August 2, 1861. Sergeant and Second Lieutenant Company I, 11th Rhode Island Volunteers, October 1, 1862—July 13, 1863.

CHARLES W RHODES,

> Private Company C, 1st Rhode Island Volunteers, May 2,—August 2, 1861.

CHRISTOPHER RHODES,

> Private Company D, 10th Rhode Island Volunteers, May 26, —September 1, 1862.

ALBERT O. ROBBINS,

> Private Troop B, 1st Rhode Island Cavalry, December 20, 1861. Assistant Surgeon, 2d Rhode Island Volunteers, November, 1863. Resigned January, 1864.

EDWARD H. SEARS,

> First Lieutenant Company D, 2d Rhode Island Volunteers, June 6, 1861. Captain Company D, July 22, 1861. Resigned October 18, 1861. First Lieutenant Battery G, 1st Rhode Island Light Artillery, October 19, 1861. Resigned November 14, 1862. Acting Assistant Paymaster United States Navy, August 27, 1863.

JOHN TETLOW, JR.,

Corporal Company B, 10th Rhode Island Volunteers, May 26,
—September 1, 1862. Captain Company I, Rhode Island
Detached Militia, on special United States service at Bonnet Point, Narragansett Bay, June, 1863. Mustered out, July,
1863.

CHARLES H. TILLINGHAST,

Acting Ensign United States Navy.

JOSEPH C. WHITING, JR.,

Corporal Company E, 10th Rhode Island Volunteers, May 26,
—September 1, 1862. Adjutant 14th Rhode Island Heavy
Artillery (colored), September 14, 1863—October 2, 1865.

CLASS OF 1856.

ALLEN BAKER, JR.,

First Lieutenant Troop B, 1st Rhode Island Cavalry, Decem-
ber 14, 1861. Captain Troop E, July 15, 1862. Wounded
March 17, 1863. Transferred to Troop D, new organization,
December 21, 1864.

HENRY R. BARKER,

Sergeant Company I, 10th Rhode Island Volunteers, May 26,
—September 1, 1862.

C. HENRY BARNEY,

Private Company A, 5th Rhode Island Heavy Artillery, December 16, 1861. Promoted to Corporal and Sergeant. Discharged January 14, 1864, to receive commission in 14th
Rhode Island Heavy Artillery (colored). Second Lieutenant
and First Lieutenant Company F, 14th R. I. H. A., December 2, 1863—October 2, 1865.

GEORGE B. BARROWS,

Private Company D, 10th Rhode Island Volunteers, May 26,—
September 1, 1862.

CHARLES H. CLARK,

Corporal Battery A, 1st Rhode Island Light Artillery, June
6, 1861. Second Lieutenant Battery C, September 13, 1861.
Resigned August 25, 1862.

CHARLES C. CRAGIN,
Private Company B, 10th Rhode Island Volunteers, May 26, —September 1, 1862. Private Company D, 2d Rhode Island Volunteers, October 8, 1863—December 8, 1863. Captain Company F, 14th Rhode Island Heavy Artillery (colored), December 5, 1863—October 2, 1865.

WILLIAM E. CLARKE,
Company C, 11th Rhode Island Volunteers. Second Lieutenant Company A, October 1, 1862. First Lieutenant and Aid-de-Camp on staff of Brigadier-General Slough, Alexandria, Va., March 6,—June 20, 1863. Mustered out July 13, 1863.

SAMUEL R. DORRANCE,
Sergeant Company D, 10th Rhode Island Volunteers, May 26, 1862. Honorably discharged July 15, 1862.

CHARLES D. OWEN,
First Lieutenant Battery A, 1st Rhode Island Light Artillery, December 2, 1861. Captain Battery G, December 21, 1861. Resigned December 24, 1862.

ROBERT H. PAINE,
Private Company D, 10th Rhode Island Volunteers, May 26, —September 1, 1862.

SUMNER U. SHEARMAN,
Second Lieutenant 4th Rhode Island Volunteers, August 27, 1862. First Lieutenant, November 25, 1862. Captain, March 7, 1863. Captured before Petersburg, Va., July 30, 1864. A prisoner at Columbia, S. C. Exchanged December 7, 1864. Mustered out December 17, 1864.

CLASS OF 1857.

JOHN H. APPLETON,
Color Corporal Company I, Rhode Island Detached Militia, on special United States service at Bonnet Point, Narragansett Bay, June, 1863. Mustered out July, 1863.

DAVID S. BOSTWICK,

    Acting Assistant Paymaster United States Navy, November 17, 1863—October 1, 1865.

FREDERICK G. CHAFFIN,

    Private Company H, 10th Rhode Island Volunteers, May 26, —September 1, 1862.

EDWARD E. CHASE,

    Sergeant-Major 1st Rhode Island Cavalry, December 14, 1861. First Lieutenant Troop E, August 4, 1862. Captain Troop H, February 14, 1863. Taken prisoner June 18, 1863. Exchanged, and mustered out March 1, 1865.

FRANK A. CHURCH,

    Private Company K, 10th Rhode Island Volunteers, May 26, —September 1, 1862.

WALTER H. COLEMAN,

    Aid-de-Camp on Staff of Governor Sprague in early part of war, 1861 and 1862. Through the Peninsula Campaign, attached to the Headquarters of General Commanding Army of Potomac, where Governor Sprague, by authority of the War Department had a staff officer present.

HARRY C. CUSHING,

    Corporal Battery A, 1st Rhode Island Light Artillery, June 6, 1861. Second Lieutenant Battery F, 4th United States Artillery, November 1, 1861. First Lieutenant Battery H, 4th United States Artillery. Brevet and First Lieutenant United States Army. Brevet Captain United States Army. Brevet Major United States Army. Still in the service.

JOHN K. DORRANCE,

    Private Company D, 10th Rhode Island Volunteers, May 26 —September 1, 1862. Second Lieutenant Company E, 2d Rhode Island Volunteers, September 15, 1864. First Lieutenant Company E, December 5, 1864. Wounded before Petersburg, Va., April 2, 1865. Brevet First Lieutenant April 2, 1865. Brevet Captain and mustered out June 20, 1865.

7

CHARLES P GAY,

>Sergeant Company H, 10th Rhode Island Volunteers, May 26, —September 1, 1862. Second Lieutenant Company A, 14th Rhode Island Heavy Artillery (colored), October 10, 1863. Resigned April 17, 1864.

ALBERT E. HAM,

>Private Company D, 10th Rhode Island Volunteers, May 26,— September 1, 1862.

EDWARD G. KING,

>Private Company D, 10th Rhode Island Volunteers, May 26, 1862. Honorably discharged June, 1862.

LUCIEN E. KENT,

>Private Company D, 10th Rhode Island Volunteers, May 26, —September 1, 1862. Also in United States Navy.

CARLO MAURAN,

>Private Company K, 10th Rhode Island Volunteers, May 26, —September 1, 1862.

GEORGE B. PECK, JR.,

>Second Lieutenant Company G, 2d Rhode Island Volunteers, December 13, 1864. Wounded at the Battle of Sailors' Creek, near Petersburg, Va., April 6, 1865. Resigned and mustered out June 30, 1865.

CHARLES S. TREAT,

>First Lieutenant and Adjutant Troop E, 1st Rhode Island Cavalry, December 16, 1661. Resigned May 30, 1862.

GEORGE W VAN SLYCK,

>Captain 128th New York Volunteers, July, 1862. Major, July, 1864. Wounded at Port Hudson, and honorably discharged May, 1865.

WILLIAM A. WILSON,

>Private Company A, 1st Rhode Island Volunteers, May 2,— August 2, 1861. Sergeant Company K, 10th Rhode Island Volunteers, May 26,—September 1, 1862. Private Company E, 11th Rhode Island Volunteers, October 1, 1862—July 13, 1863.

IRA R. WILBUR,

Corporal Company E, 10th Rhode Island Volunteers, May 26, —September 1, 1862.

CLASS OF 1858.

JOHN R. BARTLETT, JR.,

Midshipman United States Navy, November 25, 1859. On duty 1861, under Admiral Farragut at New Orleans. Ensign September 8, 1863, on Staff Admiral Dahlgren. Lieutenant February 22, 1864, under Admiral Porter. Commanded sailors in assault on Fort Fisher, and was presented with a vote of thanks by the General Assembly of Rhode Island for his part in that victory. Lieutenant-Commander July 25, 1866. Commander April 25, 1877. Now in command of United States Coast Survey Steamer Blake.

GEORGE T. BAKER,

Corporal Company B, 10th Rhode Island Volunteers, May 26, —September 1, 1862.

J. NELSON BOGMAN,

Corporal Company M, Third Rhode Island Heavy Artillery, March 17, 1862 Mortally wounded October 22, 1862, in action at Pocotaligo, S. C., and died October 25, from his wounds at Port Royal, S. C.

ZEPHANIAH BROWN, 2D,

Corporal Company K, 10th Rhode Island Volunteers, May 26, —September 1, 1862. First Lieutenant Company D, 14th Rhode Island Heavy Artillery (colored), October 24, 1863. Acting Adjutant 1st Battalion. Resigned June 1, 1865.

SAMUEL S. DAVIS,

Private Company D, 10th Rhode Island Volunteers, May 26, —September 1, 1862.

PETER HUNT,

Sergeant-Major Battery C, 1st Rhode Island Light Artillery, August, 1861. Second Lieutenant Battery A. October, 1862. First Lieutenant Battery A, November, 1862. Mortally wounded at Battle of Cold Harbor, Va., May 30, 1864. Died in Washington, D. C., June 14, 1864.

CHARLES G. INGRAHAM,

Sergeant Company F, 10th Rhode Island Volunteers, May 26, —September 1, 1862.

HENRY H. METCALF,

Private Company C, 3d Rhode Island Heavy Artillery, January 1, 1862; Sergeant, May 1; First Sergeant, September 7, 1862; Second Lieutenant, November 28, 1862; First Lieutenant, April 24, 1863. Mustered out March 17, 1865.

PEYTON H. RANDOLPH,

Private Company F, 1st Rhode Island Volunteers, May 2,— August 2, 1861. Volunteer Officer United States Navy, November 11, 1863—October 21, 1865.

HENRY C. SALISBURY,

United States Navy.

CHARLES L. STAFFORD,

Sergeant Company B, 10th Rhode Island Volunteers, May 26, —September 1, 1862. Second Lieutenant Company B, 14th Rhode Island Heavy Artillery (colored), May 15, 1863. First Lieutenant Company I, and Battalion Adjutant, May 11,— October 2, 1865.

FRANK A. WATERMAN,

Sergeant Battery D, 1st Rhode Island Light Artillery, September 4, 1861. Second Lieutenant Battery G, July 14, 1864. First Lieutenant Battery F, May 16, 1865, and mustered out July 14, 1865.

CLASS OF 1859.

WILLIAM F ATWOOD,

Private Company A, 10th Rhode Island Volunteers, May 26, 1862. Died in Washington, D. C., June 28, 1862.

NATHAN H. BAKER,

Corporal Company B, 10th Rhode Island Volunteers, May 26, September 1, 1862.

JOSEPH D. BROOKS,
Private Company E, 11th Rhode Island Volunteers, October 1, 1862, July 13, 1863.

JAMES W BLACKWOOD,
Private Company B, 10th Rhode Island Volunteers, May 26, —September 1, 1862.

WILLIAM V CARR,
First Lieutenant Company G, 2d Regiment Rhode Island Volunteers, February 10, 1865. Captain Company G, July 11, 1865, and mustered out July 13, 1865.

WILLIAM P. CRAGIN,
Private Company B, 10th Rhode Island Volunteers, May 26, —September 1, 1862.

JESSE P. EDDY,
Corporal Company K, 10th Rhode Island Volunteers, May 26, —September 1, 1862.

FRANK FROST,
Private Company B, 10th Rhode Island Volunteers, May 26,— September 1, 1862. Private Company D, 11th Rhode Island Volunteers, October 1, 1862—July 13, 1863. Second Lieutenant Company M, 14th Rhode Island Heavy Artillery (colored), December 24, 1863—June 14, 1865.

CHARLES B. GREENE,
Private Company B, 10th Rhode Island Volunteers, May 26, —September 1, 1862. Private Company I, 11th Rhode Island Volunteers, October 1, 1862—July 13, 1863.

BENJAMIN E. KELLY,
Private Company C, 1st Rhode Island Volunteers, May 2,— August 1, 1861. First Sergeant and Sergeant-Major Battery G, 1st Rhode Island Light Artillery, December 2, 1861. Second Lieutenant Battery G, November 18, 1862, for gallantry at the Battle of Antietam. Killed at the second Battle of Fredericksburg Va., May 3, 1863.

JOHN B. KELLY,
> Corporal Company B, 10th Rhode Island Volunteers, May 26, —September 2, 1862. First Sergeant Company I, 11th Rhode Island Volunteers, October 1, 1863—July 13, 1863.

JOHN E. LARNED, JR.,
> Private Company H, 10th Rhode Island Volunteers, May 26,— September 1, 1862.

CHARLES M. LATHAM,
> Private Company B, 10th Rhode Island Volunteers, May 26,— September 1, 1862. In Signal Corps. Died in the service.

GEORGE F MANN.
> Private Company K, 6th Independent New York Horse Artillery, October 5, 1861—1864.

GEORGE F ORMSBEE,
> United States Navy.

WILLIAM K. POTTER,
> Private Company I, 11th Rhode Island Volunteers, October 1, 1862—July 13, 1863.

DANA B. ROBINSON,
> Private Company B, 10th Rhode Island Volunteers, May 26, —September 1, 1862.

GEORGE H. SPARHAWK,
> Private Company B, 10th Rhode Island Volunteers, May 26, —September 1, 1862. Corporal Company I, 11th Rhode Island Volunteers, October 1, 1862—July 13, 1863.

WILLIAM A. SPICER,
> Private Company B, 10th Rhode Island Volunteers, May 26, 1862. Detached on special service at Headquarters Army of Virginia, July 2, 1862. Mustered out September 1, 1862.

CLASS OF 1860.

CHARLES H. ANTHONY,
> Private Company B, 10th Rhode Island Volunteers, May 26,— September 1, 1862.

HORACE K. BLANCHARD,

Private Company B, 10th Rhode Island Volunteers, May 26, September 1, 1862.

ARTHUR W DENNIS,

Adjutant-General's office, Rhode Island, 1862—1863. Deputy Provost Marshal, Oregon, June, 1863. Mustered out in 1865.

JAMES F FIELD,

Private Company B, 10th Rhode Island Volunteers, May 26,— September 1, 1862.

EDWIN B. FISKE,

Private Company B, 10th Rhode Island Volunteers, May, 26, —September 1, 1862.

WILLIAM A. H. GRANT,

Corporal Company E, 10th Rhode Island Volunteers, May 26, —September 1, 1862.

DAVID HUNT, JR.,

Private Company B, 10th Rhode Island Volunteers, May 26. Honorably discharged June, 1862.

J. WILSON MCCRILLIS,

Private Company K, 10th Rhode Island Volunteers, May 26, 1862. Honorably discharged June, 1862.

SAMUEL T. MITCHELL,

Private Company K, 10th Rhode Island Volunteers, May 26,— —September 1, 1862. Company C, 11th Rhode Island Volunteers, October 1, 1862—July 13, 1863.

FENNER H. PECKHAM, JR.,

Private Company E, 3d Rhode Island Heavy Artillery, November 6, 1861. Detached as Acting Assistant Hospital Steward, December 1, 1861—December 31, 1862. Second Lieutenant Companies B, H, and I, 12th Rhode Island Volunteers, December 31, 1862—March 7, 1863. Resigned July 29, 1863.

JOHN A. REYNOLDS,

> Private Company B, 10th Rhode Island Volunteers, May 26,— September 1, 1862. Corporal Company I, 11th Rhode Island Volunteers, October 1, 1862—July 13, 1863. Second Lieutenant Company F, 14th Rhode Island Heavy Artillery (colored), December 23, 1863—October 2, 1865.

HOWARD O. STURGES,

> Corporal Company D, 10th Rhode Island Volunteers, May 26,—September 1, 1862.

FRANK F. TINGLEY,

> Private Company B, 10th Rhode Island Volunteers, May 26. Honorably discharged June, 1862.

WILLIAM P VAUGHAN,

> Corporal Company B, 10th Rhode Island Volunteers, May 26, —September 1, 1862.

CLASS OF 1861.

DANIEL BUSH,

> Corporal Company D, 10th Rhode Island Volunteers, May 26, September 1, 1862. Second Lieutenant Company B, 11th Rhode Island Volunteers, October 1, 1862. First Lieutenant Company H, April 14, 1863. Mustered out July 13, 1863.

JESSE M. BUSH,

> Private Company B, 10th Rhode Island Volunteers, May 26,— September 1, 1862.

FREDERICK W GRANGER

> Private 10th Rhode Island Battery, May 26,—August 30, 1862.

CHARLES T. GREENE,

> Private Company B, 10th Rhode Island Volunteers, May 26, —September 1, 1862. Private and Sergeant 3d Rhode Island Cavalry, March 14,—June 7, 1864. Second Lieutenant Company A, 14th Rhode Island Heavy Artillery, July 12, 1864—October 2, 1865.

CHARLES L. HODGES,

> 25th United States Infantry

WILLIAM D. MASON,

Served in Signal Corps, United States Army, April 4, 1864—August 26, 1865.

FREDERICK METCALF,

Enlisted as a private in Company B, 10th Rhode Island Volunteers, May 26, 1862. Not mustered, being only 15 years of age. Second Lieutenant 3d Rhode Island Heavy Artillery, October, 1863. Post-Adjutant, Fort Pulaski, Georgia. First Lieutenant May 27, 1864. Died at Beaufort, S. C., August 28, 1864, in the seventeenth year of his age.

BROCKHOLST MATHEWSON, 2D,

Corporal Company D, 10th Rhode Island Volunteers, May 26, —September 1, 1862.

EUGENE F PHILLIPS,

Corporal Company A, 10th Rhode Island Volunteers, May 26, —September 1, 1862.

JOHN R. READ,

Corporal Company I, 11th Rhode Island Volunteers, October 1, 1862—July 13, 1863.

CHARLES M. SMITH,

Private Company D, 10th Rhode Island Volunteers, May 26,—September 1, 1862. Second Lieutenant Company L, 14th Rhode Island Heavy Artillery, January 30, 1864. Mustered out October 2, 1865.

CLASS OF 1862.

HARRY A. RICHARDSON,

Company K, 9th Rhode Island Volunteers, May 26,—September 2, 1862.

CLASS OF 1863.

JAMES C. BUTTERWORTH, JR.,

Enlisted as Private in Providence Marine Corps Artillery, for special United States service at Bonnet Point, Narragansett Bay, June 1863. Mustered out July, 1863.

EUGENE F GRANGER,

> New Hampshire Volunteers. Missing and reported to have died in prison at Salisbury, N. C.

RICHARD E. THOMPSON,

> Enlisted as Private in Providence Marine Corps Artillery, for special United States service at Bonnet Point, Narragansett Bay, June, 1863. Mustered out July, 1863. Now an officer in United States Infantry.

---◆---

NOTE.

The utmost care has been taken to make the list published on the preceding pages, accurate and complete. It presents a most honorable record, and it will be a matter of regret if any names have been omitted. About one-fifth of all the boys who entered the Providence High School, from its commencement in 1843 to 1861 inclusive, served in the army or navy of the United States during the civil war; and not less than twenty-five per cent. of the classes from 1850 to 1860 inclusive, are known to have been in the service.

Number of teachers in the service, 6; number of students, 225. Number who died in the service, 17

SUMMARY.

CLASS.	NUMBER OF BOYS IN THE SCHOOL.	NUMBER IN THE SERVICE.	PERCENTAGE IN THE SERVICE.
1843,	114	11	10
1844,	65	3	5
1845,	54	7	13
1846,	60	6	10
1847,	63	5	8
1848,	53	8	15
1849,	57	12	21
1850,	54	11	20
1851,	59	13	22
1852,	52	10	19
1853,	55	20	36
1854,	39	7	18
1855,	77	23	30
1856,	48	1	23
1857,	55	18	33
1858,	68	12	18
1859,	61	19	31
1860,	65	14	22
1861,	61	11	18
Total,	1,160	221	Ave'ge, 19